Don't Touch the Kryptonite!

(Don't even THINK about it!)

Written and illustrated by

Deborah Buschgens

Email:
dlbuschgens@gmail.com
deb.mirrormirror@gmail.com
Find me at:
www.deborahbuschgens.com
go,deborahbuschgens.com

KRYPTONITE

AN INSIDIOUS GREEN SUBSTANCE.

IT IS THE **ONLY** THING CAPABLE OF STEALING YOUR SUPERPOWERS.

WestBow Press books may be ordered through booksellers or by contacting:

WestBow Press
A Division of Thomas Nelson & Zondervan
1663 Liberty Drive
Bloomington, IN 47403
www.westbowpress.com
1 (866) 928-1240

Because of the dynamic nature of the Internet, any web addresses or links contained in this book may have changed since publication and may no longer be valid. The views expressed in this work are solely those of the author and do not necessarily reflect the views of the publisher, and the publisher hereby disclaims any responsibility for them.

Any people depicted in stock imagery provided by Getty Images are models, and such images are being used for illustrative purposes only.
Certain stock imagery © Getty Images.

Scripture taken from the Amplified Bible, Copyright © 1954, 1958, 1962, 1964, 1965, 1987 by The Lockman Foundation. Used by permission.

ISBN: 978-1-9736-8116-8 (sc)
ISBN: 978-1-9736-8117-5 (e)

Library of Congress Control Number: 2019919576

Print information available on the last page.

WestBow Press rev. date: 02/24/2020

WESTBOW
PRESS®
A DIVISION OF THOMAS NELSON
& ZONDERVAN

To all the Heroes in my life!
And to Cooper,
My fluffy friend.

*A*nd immediately Jesus stretched out *His* hand and caught him, and said to him,

"O you of little **faith**, why did you *doubt*?"

Matthew 14:31 (NKJV) *Emphasis Mine*

For though we walk (live) in the flesh, we are not carrying on our warfare according to the flesh and using mere human weapons.

2 Corinthians 10:3 (AMP)

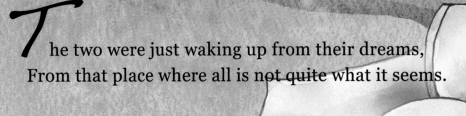

*T*he two were just waking up from their dreams,
From that place where all is not quite what it seems.

The blonde-headed girl and her white, fluffy friend
Realized their sleep had just come to an end.

But before they had chance to open their eyes,
The girl heard a voice. It was such a surprise!

It pierced through the calm; it cut through the night ...

"Don't touch the

*S*he stretched and yawned, then climbed out of bed,
While thoughts of *kryptonite* played in her head.

Could arch enemy Satan be up to his scheming,
Planning and plotting while she lay there dreaming?

She considered that thought as she looked at her face,
Framed in ***God's Mirror***, secure in His grace.

She saw herself clearly, heart flooding with Light.

Don't touch the *kryptonite*!

ot long ago, when things seemed less bright,
She'd learned of two mirrors - of darkness and Light.

The *World* was the one, ***God's Kingdom*** the other.
Back then she hadn't known one from another!

She'd asked, "Where am I looking? What do I see?"
Then she turned to God's Mirror and she was set free!

Now she was filled with God's power and might!

Don't touch the *kryptonite*!

*A*gain she considered the words that God spoke
As she'd slipped from her dreams and slowly awoke.

She was getting a sense, though it seemed quite absurd,
Of an ominous nature to this *kryptonite* word.

A green, threatening cloud sneaking up from behind,
With power to confuse and take over your mind!

"Okay", she decided, "that's it, that's enough!"
She made mental note not to touch the green stuff.

S he enjoyed her fine breakfast of oats and molasses,
Then donned her red cape and designer sunglasses.

With the friend close beside her, assuming his place,
She greeted the world, a smile crossing her face.

Heart beating faster, she looked toward the day,
Waiting to hear what the Spirit would say.

She had great expectations, with hopes of rebirth,
Of releasing God's Kingdom; bringing heaven to earth.

*T*here's power inside those who dare to believe -
A mysterious weapon tucked under their sleeve.

They have power to heal and to raise up the dead;
To set captives free and love them instead.

They are one with God's Spirit, He lives right inside.
When they focus on Jesus the devil can't hide.

They team up as one to destroy evil on sight! But,

Don't touch the *kryptonite!*

*T*o the *World's* pattern she has not conformed,
Seeing now in *God's Kingdom*, she's being transformed!

She'd sat down with God for days and had learned
That the real things in life are spiritually discerned.

It's a new way of seeing, in's out and up's down,
The unseen more real than the things all around.

So now as she prays, because she's God's daughter,
The Kingdom pours out of her spirit like water!

With rivers of Life flowing out of her being,
The astounding, miraculous things she is seeing!

Sharing *God's Message* and binding up sickness,
Qualified and anointed as God is her witness.

He gives her the power and they work as a team
To bring Light into darkness, as if in a dream.

They release healing and hope - oh it's so fun
To destroy and undo what the devil has done!

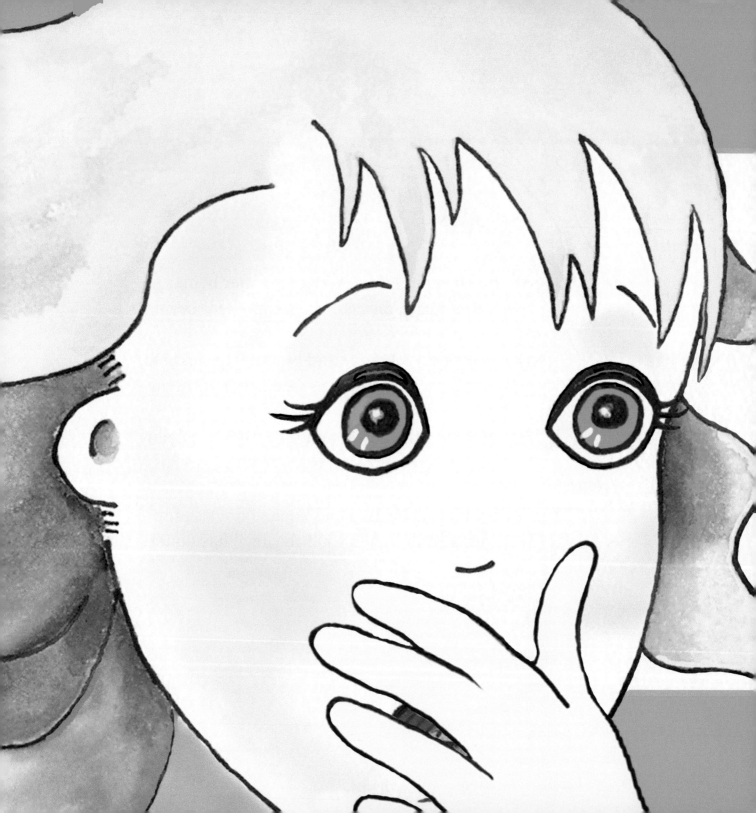

A superhero she is, bringing sight to the blind,
Fighting crime and injustice, freeing mankind!

And just when she thinks she is done for the day,
A *greenish* thought whispers,

"Did God really say ...?"

It caused her to pause, to just think for a second.
She pushed it away but still the thought beckoned.

She pondered the words and realized with fright,
She'd just touched the *kryptonite*!

She felt herself weaken, *doubt* clouded her mind,
Draining her power, belief and sound mind.

Then hearing a noise, she saw in sheer horror
A pack of wild dogs fiercely rounding the corner!

Running and snarling they ran straight toward her,
Crowding and jumping they meant to destroy her!

Her heart skipped a beat; she looked wildly around.
Then she saw Jesus, calmly standing His ground.

He stood within reach, beyond the bedlam and dust
Of vicious dogs leaping in malice and lust.

His eyes drew her in and she understood clearly,
Diverting her gaze would cost her most dearly.

Her heart slowed and calmed, she connected with Jesus,
God's Kingdom moved in, she was not ripped to pieces.

One by one they lost interest, the dogs lost their moment,
Skulking away from their stronger opponent.

Then the atmosphere changed, she was standing alone,
Left to wonder what happened, shaken right to the bone.

It began with a thought whispered in her right ear,
Speaking the *lie* that then filled her with *fear*.

This unleashed the dogs at that time without warning,
But hadn't God spoken about that just this morning?

She connected the dots; *doubt* made the dogs bite!

Ah, this must be *kryptonite*!

She sat down with the friend to gather her thoughts,
To thoroughly think through the do's and should not's.

She knew who she was and was doing so well,
Then the thought came, releasing the hound dogs from hell!

Words whispered from Satan were shrewd and so sly,
Presuming to tell her *God's Word* was a lie!

He roams around looking for those to devour,
Knowing just the right day; just the right hour.

*H*e speaks through our thoughts; it's his weapon of choice,
Using *doubt*, *fear* and *shame* to silence our voice.

Take time to look closely and I think you might find,
That the battle takes place on the screen in your mind.

A thought leads to reflection, then changes the way
We go about business in the course of our day.

Satan fears our conviction, of what we can achieve,
Of the *power* we have when we truly believe.

*H*er *faith* was returning, she felt so much stronger,
Though she couldn't contain herself very much longer.

She straightened her cape, gave the small friend a pat,
Then turned to her Dad for a heart to heart chat.

"Lord", she cried out, "there's so much I'm learning!"
She could feel God's Spirit within her heart burning.

"The enemy attacks us with *fear*, *wounds* and *lies*.
I must also have weapons!" She could only surmise.

"My fight's not against people," she thought, overwhelmed,
"But against spiritual forces in the heavenly realm.

I'm not of the *World,* but the ***Kingdom of God,***
So the weapons I use might just seem a bit odd.

I'll take my thoughts captive to Jesus and see
A fresh pathway appear - a clear strategy.

With a view way up high I am seated with Him,
Where all of my problems now seem rather dim."

When you feel a thought coming, before it is heard,
Check if it matches up with God and His Word.

Satan says things to scare, hurt you and more -
Guilt, *condemnation*; *thoughts to even the score*.

Discernment is much like a force field you know,
Making it clear what's to stay and to GO!

When the devil comes near and his voice starts to yap,
Swing into action with a POW!, BAM! and ...

zap!

*F*ight *his* words with *God's Word*, *as that* is your sword,
He's there in the battle, for He is your Lord!

He gave you His armor to guard your well-being. Worn with assurance, there's no need for fleeing.

Righteousness your breastplate,
Faith as your shield, Feet shod in *Peace*, you're fashionably well heeled!

The helmet of *Salvation*, protecting your mind,
And the belt of *Truth* to gird up your spine.

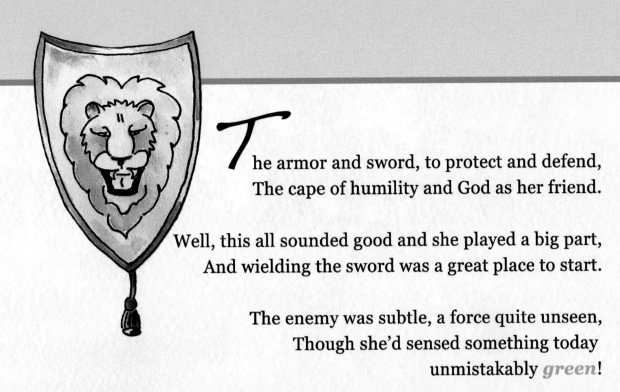

*T*he armor and sword, to protect and defend,
The cape of humility and God as her friend.

Well, this all sounded good and she played a big part,
And wielding the sword was a great place to start.

The enemy was subtle, a force quite unseen,
Though she'd sensed something today
unmistakably *green*!

She'd had a close call; it had been such a fright,

Don't touch the *kryptonite*!

*A*s she made her way home to get in from the cold,
Clear visions from God began to unfold.

She saw a cool tool belt that was filled to the max.
Each tool had a purpose, the bow, arrow and axe.

Like *worship* and *praise*,
forgiveness, *thanksgiving*,
Giving your all to the life that you're living.

Thinking on things that are true, worthy and right,

And NOT getting close
to the *kryptonite*!

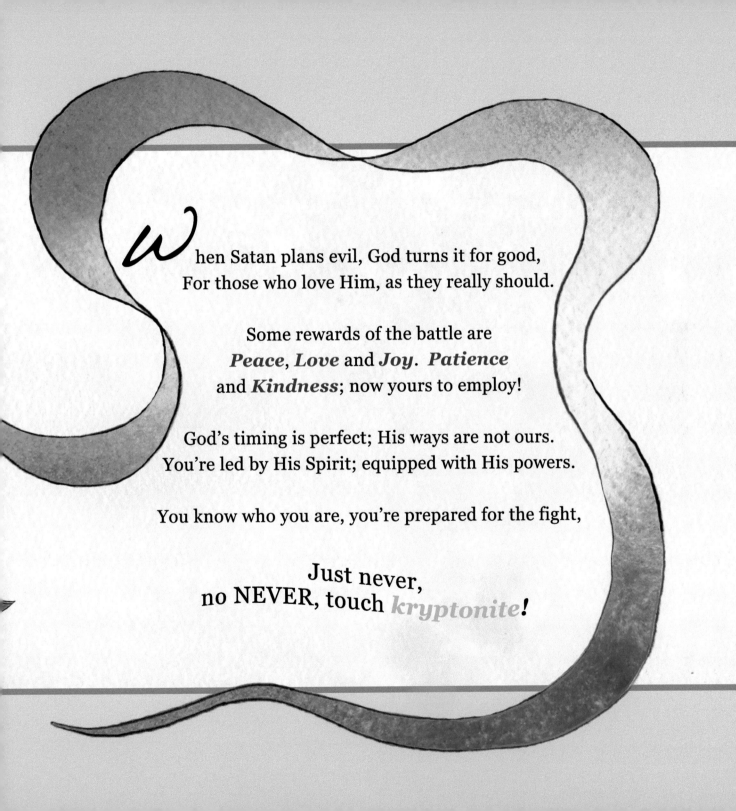

When Satan plans evil, God turns it for good,
For those who love Him, as they really should.

Some rewards of the battle are
Peace, *Love* and *Joy*. *Patience*
and *Kindness*; now yours to employ!

God's timing is perfect; His ways are not ours.
You're led by His Spirit; equipped with His powers.

You know who you are, you're prepared for the fight,

Just never,
no NEVER, touch *kryptonite*!

DON'T

TOUCH THE

KRYPTONITE!

(DON'T EVEN *THINK* ABOUT IT!)

Deborah was born in Calgary, Canada. She received her Bachelor of Education through the University of Calgary and art training through the Alberta College of Art. Deborah is very interested in how God speaks prophetically through dreams and visions; how He connects encounter with God with the Word of God. This story was woven together through such encounters and scripture to reveal our hidden authority and identity in Christ.

Printed in the United States
By Bookmasters